The Power of A Wife's Heart to Honor,
Heal and Bring Hope

THE HEART OF
THE HOME

Foreword

Rev. Dr. Candace Kelly

JOYCE KITCHEN

The Heart of the Home

Printed and bound in the United States of America

Published by Cole Publishing

Library of Congress
Cataloging-in-Publication Data
ISBN: 979-8-9885825-8-8

Cole Publishing
4067 Hardwick Street #282
Lakewood, CA 90712

Email: Colepublishing2000@gmail.com
Book Cover Design by Cole Publishing Company

For Book Orders:
Contact us at Cole Publishing Company
www.ColePublishing.org

Cole Publishing

CONTENTS

DEDICATION V

ACKNOWLEDGMENTS VII

FOREWORD. IX

INTRODUCTION
GIVING LIFE TO THE HOME 11

CHAPTER 1
Communications from the Heart 15

CHAPTER 2
Building Our Husbands Up 21

CHAPTER 3
The Covenant of Marriage and Forgiveness 25

CHAPTER 4
Loving our Husbands Unconditionally 29

CHAPTER 5
Reverencing Our Husbands 33

CHAPTER 6
Financial Harmony – A Foundation for Peace in Marriage 37

CHAPTER 7
A Role Model of God-Likeness 41

CHAPTER 8
Conclusion: Building a Christ-Centered Marriage 45

COUPLE OR GROUP QUESTIONS
FOR REFLECTION AND DISCUSSION 49

ABOUT THE AUTHOR
Reverend Joyce Reece Kitchen 53

DEDICATION

This book is dedicated to Jesus Christ, my Savior and Lord. Without His inspiration and guidance, this book would have remained an unrealized dream. I'm grateful for the knowledge, wisdom, and experience He gifted me with, and for the blessing of sharing it with so many others.

The second dedication is to my husband, Maurice, who partners with me to live out the words on the pages of this book.

ACKNOWLEDGMENTS

After giving honor to God, next is my "baby Sis," Rev. Dr. Candace Kelly. Without Dr. Kelly, the pages in this book would have remained in my file drawer. She has persevered for twenty years to get me to birth this work. I also thank my sister Maurine and her husband Greg, who have been faithful, Christian models of what marriage should be over the past fifty-plus years.

There is not enough room to mention all of the writings and teachings on marriage that have inspired me over the years. Finally, I am so grateful for the couples who have trusted me to provide premarital and marital counseling using the gifts and talents God has blessed me with.

FOREWORD

Home is more than just walls and a roof—it is the sacred space where love dwells, faith is nurtured, and relationships are refined. At the heart of every home is the divine calling to cultivate peace, unity, and understanding. In *The Heart of the Home*, Joyce Kitchen brings forth a message that is both timeless and transformational, guiding couples toward deeper connection, biblical wisdom, and God-centered communication.

Kitchen's insight is not just theoretical but deeply rooted in Scripture, experience, and a profound understanding of God's design for marriage. In today's world, where relationships are often strained by busyness, miscommunication, and unspoken expectations, this book serves as a lighthouse—offering guidance, encouragement, and practical wisdom to those seeking a thriving, Christ-honoring marriage.

With warmth, grace, and a shepherd's heart, Kitchen reminds us that the foundation of any strong relationship is communication—not just the words we speak, but the love, respect, and intentionality behind them. She masterfully weaves biblical principles with real-life application, ensuring that every reader walks away equipped to nurture a home filled with peace, mutual respect, and God's abiding presence.

Whether you are newly married, have been on the journey for decades, or are seeking healing and restoration in your relationship, *The Heart of the Home* will encourage and challenge you to build a marriage that reflects the love of Christ. May this book be a source of inspiration, helping you create a home where faith flourishes, love abounds, and God remains at the center.

Rev. Dr. Candace Kelly

President and CEO
Cole Publishing Company & Consultatnts

INTRODUCTION
GIVING LIFE TO THE HOME

The Heart of the Home: A Divine Calling

The heart is the vital organ that sustains and gives life, pumping blood to every part of our bodies and ensuring that each part functions properly. In much the same way, women are divinely positioned as the heart of the home, the source of love, warmth, and emotional support. While husbands are called to be the head, the leader of the household, the wife holds the role of nurturing, sustaining, and breathing life into the family dynamic. As the heart sustains the body, a woman sustains the home, creating a haven where love, care, and faith can flourish. This is

A body can be kept alive if the brain dies, but if the heart dies, everything dies with it.

a vitally important role. A body can be kept alive if the brain dies, but if the heart dies, everything dies with it.

In Scripture, we find that the home is meant to be a place of peace, stability, and divine order. When we align ourselves with God's design for the family, we cultivate a home that honors Him and nurtures each member. Yet many times we fall short of this ideal, and as a result, we witness brokenness in marriages, fractured families, and weakened communities. It is crucial, then, for women to understand and embrace their sacred calling as the heart of the home, and to live in accordance with the divine blueprint God has established for the family.

The Divine Order: Understanding Our Roles

God in His infinite wisdom has ordained an order within the family. This divine order is not meant to oppress or diminish one's worth but rather to promote harmony, purpose, and mutual support. Ephesians 5:22-23 tells us, "Wives, submit to your own husbands, as to the Lord. For the husband is the head of the wife, as also Christ is the head of the church; and He is the Savior of the body." The husband is called to be the head of the home, responsible for leadership, protection, and provision, while the wife is called to be the heart, responsible for nurturing, supporting, and bringing life.

These roles are complementary, not competitive. The husband leads, but the wife empowers, strengthens, and sustains him. As Proverbs 31:10-12 describes, "Who can find a virtuous woman? For her price is far above rubies. The heart of her husband doth safely trust in her, so that he shall have no need of spoil." A godly woman's support and love empower her husband to fulfill his role as the head, creating a home where both can thrive in their respective roles.

However, fulfilling this divine order requires a relationship with God. As 1 John 4:7-8 reminds us, "Beloved, let us love one another, for love is of God; and everyone who loves is born of God and knows God. He who does not love does not know God, for God is love." Our relationship with God is the foundation upon which we build our marriages. It is from His abundant love that we draw the strength to love our husbands sacrificially and selflessly, fulfilling our role as the heart of the home.

A Love That Reflects God's Love

God's love is sacrificial, unconditional, and boundless. It is the love that sent His Son, Jesus Christ, to the cross to atone for our sins. As women, we are called to reflect this same love in our marriages: a love that gives without expecting anything in return, a love that sacrifices for the good of others, and a love that endures through hardship and pain.

This sacrificial love is not always easy. It requires selflessness and a willingness to put the needs of others before our own. When my husband, Ronald, asked me to marry him, I sought God's will. He spoke a word that still resonates with me today: *"It will be fine as long as you are willing to give 100%."* At the time, I interpreted this as God's confirmation that I should proceed with the marriage, but in hindsight, I now realize that God was preparing me for the weight and responsibility of being the heart of the home. He was calling me to a life of selflessness and sacrificial love.

The role of the wife as the heart of the home demands full commitment. It requires giving, even when it is difficult, even when you feel drained, and even when your husband does not seem to deserve it. This kind of love demands time, energy, and effort. It is a daily choice to serve, to encourage, to forgive, and to love with the same intensity with which God loves us. As wives, we are called to reflect God's love in our actions, words, and deeds.

The Call to Build, Not Tear Down

A wife's role as the heart of the home is also to build her husband up, not tear him down. When we align ourselves with God's plan, we begin to see our marriage through a divine lens. We no longer measure our relationship based on what we receive but on what we give. We focus not on the faults and imperfections of our husbands, but on the potential within them. As Proverbs 14:1 states, "The wise woman builds her house, but the foolish pulls it down with her hands." The heart of the home is meant to build, nurture, and strengthen, not destroy.

Here are a few biblical principles to guide the process of building up, rather than tearing down:

> **Building Up**: Speak words of encouragement and affirmation to your husband. Proverbs 31:26 says, "She opens her mouth with wisdom, and on her tongue is the law of kindness." Our words have the power to either build up or tear down. Let us use them to build up our husbands and families.

> **Forgiving Freely:** Forgiveness is a key element in nurturing a home filled with peace. Ephesians 4:32 exhorts us, "Be kind to one another, tenderhearted, forgiving one another, even as God in Christ forgave you." By extending the grace that God gives us, we let go of past hurts and move forward in love.

> **Loving Unconditionally:** Love is not contingent on our husband's behavior or performance; it is a reflection of God's love for us. In 1 Corinthians 13:4-7, we see that love "bears all things, believes all things, hopes all things, endures all things." Even in difficult seasons, we are called to love unconditionally.

> **Thinking Selflessly:** Philippians 2:4 teaches us to "let each of you look out not only for his own interests, but also for the interests of others." A wife's role is not about seeking her own comfort, but about seeking the good of her husband and family.

> **Reverencing Your Husband:** Ephesians 5:33 commands, "Let the wife see that she respects her husband." Respect is a fundamental element of a healthy marriage. By honoring and respecting our husbands, we create an environment where love and mutual submission thrive.

Creating a Legacy of Love

As we embrace our role as the heart of the home, we breathe life into our marriages and families. We create spaces where love, joy, and peace abound, and where children grow up feeling safe, secure, and loved. Our actions and attitudes set the tone for the family dynamic. By following God's design, we can create homes that honor Him and bless those who live in them.

The journey to becoming the heart of the home is not always easy. It requires dying to self, surrendering our hearts to God, and daily choosing to love with His kind of love. But it is a journey worth taking. As we commit ourselves to this divine calling, we create not only strong marriages, but a lasting legacy of love, faithfulness, and devotion that will be passed down to future generations.

Let us remember that we are not alone in this journey. God, in His grace and wisdom, equips us for the task at hand. As we rely on His strength, we can fulfill our sacred calling as the heart of the home, building lives, homes, and families that reflect His love and glory.

Scripture References:

- Ephesians 5:22-23
- Proverbs 31:10-12
- 1 John 4:7-8
- Proverbs 14:1
- Ephesians 4:32
- 1 Corinthians 13:4-7
- Philippians 2:4
- Ephesians 5:33

CHAPTER 1

COMMUNICATIONS FROM THE HEART

C ommunication stands as the cornerstone of the husband-wife relationship. Without it, even the most foundational aspects of the relationship—love, respect, intimacy, and understanding—are vulnerable to breakdown, leading to conflict, chaos, and eventual failure. Yet, when good communication is present, even the most challenging situations can be navigated, reconciled, and resolved.

The Prerequisites of Communication: Respect and Acceptance

The bedrock of effective communication is rooted in two essential virtues: **respect and acceptance.** We must honor our husbands as individuals created in God's image, endowed with His Spirit (Genesis 1:27). This recognition allows us to embrace their differences—not as flaws but as part of God's divine design. Men, like women, have distinct perspectives, likes, dislikes, ways of thinking, acting, and feeling. Respecting them as separate persons with unique attributes fosters a healthy and productive dialogue.

Respecting our husbands involves acknowledging their right to be different from us. This means resisting the urge to manipulate them or try to control their behaviors through subtle language or demands. Instead of using phrases like, "you should" or "you need to," which often position us as the ones who know best, we should approach them with a humble attitude, seeking to understand rather than control. Manipulation—whether intentional or not—erodes trust and breeds resistance, as it undermines their sense of autonomy.

Scripture calls us to honor one another (Romans 12:10), a principle that must govern our communication. Ephesians 4:29 encourages us to speak in ways that build up rather than tear down. Respectful communication is not just about the words we use but also the tone with which we say them. The tone can either encourage openness or close down the conversation.

Speaking the Truth in Love

When we communicate with our husbands, we are urged to "speak the truth in love" (Ephesians 4:15). This requires deep spiritual maturity. Speaking the truth in love means offering correction or insight, but doing so with gentleness and kindness, mindful of the other person's heart and needs. It is not about "winning" an argument but about honoring God and our spouse through the way we converse.

For example, if it is necessary to bring up a painful topic, we should aim to express how we feel rather than accusing or blaming. Instead of saying, "You always come home late without telling me," we might express, "I felt worried and lonely when I did not hear from you." This approach, grounded in vulnerability, fosters understanding rather than defensiveness.

Proverbs 15:1 reminds us that "A gentle answer turns away wrath, but a harsh word stirs up anger." Thus, communicating with grace ensures that the message is received with love and respect, keeping the door open for deeper understanding.

When countries go to war, there are rules of engagement. This may be an extreme example, but it proves a point. Establishing clear rules of engagement in marriage helps couples navigate conflict with love and respect, intentionally strengthening communication and preserving their bond even in difficult moments.

Acceptance: Embracing Their Humanity

Acceptance does not mean passive approval of all actions or behaviors, but rather recognizing our husbands as imperfect human beings, just as we are. It means accepting that they will make mistakes, as will we, and allowing space for grace and growth. Romans 15:7 urges us to "accept one another, just as Christ accepted you, in order to bring praise to God."

We must never attack our husbands' character when they make mistakes. Instead, we should address the behavior and its impact on us, without attacking their identity. This is a fundamental distinction. It is one thing to say, "I was hurt by what you did," but quite another to say, "You always mess everything up!" The latter shuts down communication and pushes our husbands away, while the former opens the door for healing and reconciliation.

The Art of Listening: Understanding Beyond Words

A key aspect of communication that is often overlooked is **listening**—truly listening. Many of us are accustomed to speaking, but real intimacy is birthed in listening. To listen means to hear not just the words, but also the underlying emotions, the unspoken cues, and the body language. This requires patience, empathy, and intentionality.

James 1:19 teaches us to be "quick to listen, slow to speak, and slow to become angry." Listening well requires setting aside our own thoughts and responses long enough to truly understand where our husbands are coming from.

Building a Safe Environment for Communication

When countries go to war, there are rules of engagement. This may be an extreme example, but it proves a point. Establishing clear rules of engagement in marriage helps couples navigate conflict with love and respect, intentionally strengthening communication and preserving their bond even in difficult moments.

The following Rules of Engagement Chart can help couples in moments of conflict:

Things That Help	Things That Hinder
Active listening	Distraction
Eye contact	Interruption
Declaration of feelings	Inappropriate language or tone
Affirming the good and positives before discussing challenges	Keeping score of wrongs and including them in current challenges
Listening without interruption	Not letting the other person finish their thoughts
Being compassionate and giving the benefit of the doubt	Judging without context and understanding

A healthy marriage thrives in an atmosphere of trust and respect. 1 Peter 3:7 reminds husbands to "be considerate as you live with your wives, and treat them with respect." For wives, this means being sensitive to the delicate balance of emotional and spiritual needs within the relationship.

Practical Tools for Effective Communication

1. Pray Together

Prayer creates a sacred space where both partners can share their hearts with God and one another (Matthew 18:20).

2. Date Night

Regular quality time fosters intimacy and strengthens the bond between husband and wife (Ecclesiastes 4:9).

3. Weekly Family Meetings

Proverbs 27:17 says, "As iron sharpens iron, so one person sharpens another." These meetings should be characterized by mutual respect, gratitude, and shared goals.

You can say anything to anyone however you want...unless you want them to hear you. If you want them to hear you, you must speak in a way that they can receive it. When speaking to our husbands, this means showing respect for who they are as men of God and our spiritual covering.

Tailoring Communication for Your Husband

Effective communication requires understanding your husband's needs and communication style. Proverbs 16:23 reminds us that "The heart of the wise makes their mouths prudent, and their lips promote instruction." You can say anything to anyone however you want...unless you want them to hear you. If you want them to hear you, you must speak in a way that they can receive it. When speaking to our husbands, this means showing respect for who they are as men of God and our spiritual covering. Communication is an ongoing effort that requires constant care and attention.

Ephesians 4:2-3 says, "Be completely humble and gentle; be patient, bearing with one another in love. Make every effort to keep the unity of the

Spirit through the bond of peace." This should be the foundation of our communication in marriage—a bond of peace, humility, and love.

Scripture References

- Genesis 1:27
- Romans 12:10
- Ephesians 4:29
- Ephesians 4:15
- Proverbs 15:1
- Romans 15:7
- James 1:19
- 1 Peter 3:7
- Matthew 18:20
- Ecclesiastes 4:9
- Proverbs 27:17
- Proverbs 16:23
- Ephesians 4:2-3

CHAPTER 2

BUILDING OUR HUSBANDS UP

Understanding Our Role in Building Up Our Husbands

To build our husbands up, we must first assess what we are working with. Just as an architect evaluates the materials before constructing a building, we must understand our husbands' strengths, weaknesses, and responsibilities as the head of the home. The Bible affirms that men are called to leadership in marriage (Ephesians 5:23), a role that requires wisdom, strength, and support.

Men are often task-oriented, focusing on outcomes, while women tend to be process-oriented, emphasizing how something is achieved. This fundamental difference means that as wives, we must ask ourselves, "How do I help him maximize the task of leadership?" One way is by ensuring he has the information he needs. This involves being honest about our needs and desires, not assuming that he instinctively knows what we want.

Vulnerability and Communication

Many women desire their husbands to anticipate their needs without being told. However, this can lead to unnecessary frustration. Clear and direct communication fosters intimacy. Vulnerability in marriage can be frightening because it exposes us to potential hurt, yet it is essential for deep connection.

My husband, Ronald, often said, "Joyce, you can never steal second with your foot on first." This means that in order to gain something valuable, we must take a risk. Let me illustrate this through an experience in my own marriage:

Ronald once brought me a beautiful postcard from a trip, writing loving words on the back. Initially, I cherished it, but when I later discovered that my mother and sister also received postcards from him, I felt less special. My initial joy turned into disappointment, and rather than expressing my feelings, I withdrew. When Ronald noticed my sullen mood and missing postcard, he asked what

There can be no intimacy without honesty: intimacy can be thought of as "into me see".

was wrong. At first, I gave minimal responses, but after some prompting, I admitted my feelings of being "just one of many" rather than uniquely cherished.

Ronald reassured me that my card was distinct, chosen specifically for me, and contained personal words that set it apart. He helped me recognize that my feelings stemmed from an internal struggle of not feeling special, rather than his actual intent. By being honest about my insecurity, I allowed him to minister to my heart, strengthening our relationship. There can be no intimacy without honesty: intimacy can be thought of as "into me see".

Supporting Our Husbands' Spiritual Leadership

A husband's primary responsibility is to lead his family toward God (1 Corinthians 11:3). This means he must be spiritually nourished through prayer, Bible study, and a personal relationship with Christ. As wives, we support this by praying with and for our husbands, encouraging spiritual discussions, and cultivating a home grounded in biblical values.

Our attitudes, speech, and actions should reflect the Word of God. We are called to be our husband's helper (Genesis 2:18), not his competitor. Supporting his leadership means understanding when to step back, when to encourage, and when to lovingly challenge in a way that honors God.

Submission and Humility in Marriage

In our world today, the concept of submission is often misunderstood. Biblical submission does not mean becoming less than who God created us to be. Instead, it requires humility, recognizing that God has established roles for harmony in marriage (Colossians 3:18). A wife's submission is a voluntary act of trust in God's design, not blind obedience.

We must always keep in mind that "different" does not mean "deficient.

A key element in submission is respectful communication. We can address any concern if we approach it with openness, honesty, and appropriateness. Being open means acknowledging that our husband's perspective, though different, is valid. We must always keep in mind that "different" does not mean "deficient." Being honest means expressing truth with love, even when it feels vulnerable. Being appropriate means maintaining respect in dialogue, and treating our husband as our covering and protector.

Allowing Our Husbands to Shape and Mold Us

Our husbands, under God's guidance, play a role in shaping us. Just as iron sharpens iron (Proverbs 27:17), our husbands refine us through correction, encouragement, and love. We must be willing to receive both praise and constructive feedback, understanding that balance is key. A husband's role is not just to build us up but also to help us grow spiritually and emotionally.

Two essential characteristics of thriving marriages are the willingness to sacrifice and the ability to compromise.

For this dynamic to work, we must trust that God is using our husband to strengthen us. Marriage is a refining process where both partners learn and grow. When we embrace this, we free ourselves from resentment and cultivate a marriage where mutual respect, love, and godly leadership flourish.

Conclusion

Building up our husbands is an intentional and ongoing effort. By recognizing their leadership role, communicating honestly, supporting their spiritual walk, embracing humility, and allowing them to refine us, we create a marriage that reflects God's design. Marriage is not about competing but complementing, not about controlling but cooperating. Two essential characteristics of thriving marriages are the willingness to sacrifice and the ability to compromise. When we trust God's plan, we build a foundation of love, respect, and enduring strength in our relationship.

Scripture References

- Ephesians 5:23
- 1 Corinthians 11:3
- Genesis 2:18
- Colossians 3:18
- Proverbs 27:17
- Philippians 2:3
- 1 Peter 3:1-2
- Ecclesiastes 4:9-10

CHAPTER 3

THE COVENANT OF
MARRIAGE AND FORGIVENESS

During premarital counseling, I often liken marriage to a room with a single door and multiple windows. Once inside, both the door and windows vanish, leaving no way out. This analogy highlights the importance of commitment—when there is no option to leave, couples are more likely to resolve conflicts with patience and diligence. Viewing marriage as an unbreakable covenant fosters a mindset of endurance rather than escape. Premarital counseling helps couples develop effective communication skills and identify potential areas of conflict before they arise. When we build a strong foundation and maintain it consistently, we navigate challenges more effectively, preventing issues from escalating into crises.

Why Forgive?

As wives, we forgive our husbands first and foremost because God commands it. But beyond obedience, forgiveness fosters intimacy. Without it, emotional walls form, preventing genuine closeness. We must also extend forgiveness because we, too, are imperfect and need our husband's grace as much as they need ours. The same understanding we seek from God and others should be extended to our husbands. Forgiveness is an expression of love. In an environment of love and grace, our husbands can grow into the men God created them to be.

What Do We Need to Forgive?

We forgive our husbands for both their actions and inactions—the words they say that wound us and the words left unsaid, the things they do that hurt, and the things they neglect to do. At times, our husbands' behavior may stem from their own fears—of rejection, failure, or inadequacy. External pressures and frustrations may lead them to react in ways that hurt us. Sometimes, we may unknowingly trigger past wounds, provoking defensive reactions. In such moments, we must remember that 90% of what people do is not about us personally, but rather a reflection of their internal battles.

Neglect can also be a source of pain. However, we must remind ourselves that our husband, like us, has struggles that often have little to do with us directly. We become affected simply because we are closest to him. One of the challenges wives face is the temptation to expect their husbands to fulfill every emotional need—a burden no human can bear. While our husbands are our closest companions, God has given us Himself and a community of other safe relationships to support us.

The Process of Forgiveness

Our humanity presents us with difficult tensions. We have the tendency to press for the extremes: being more or less than human. The truth is we are just plain human, and so are our husbands. We are both fallible, hence the need for forgiveness. When we embrace the truth of our own humanity, it ought to increase our capacity to forgive.

1 John 1:9 states: "If we confess our sins, He is faithful and just and will forgive us our sins and purify us from all unrighteousness." Just as God forgives and restores us, we must ask Him for the strength to extend the same grace to our husband. When our husband has hurt us, we must create a safe space where he feels encouraged to seek forgiveness. This means adopting an attitude and language that communicates our willingness to forgive. While forgiveness is often a process, if our husband knows we are committed to that process, he will be more willing to engage in reconciliation.

God's faithfulness in forgiving us sets the standard for our own forgiveness. We must continue to love our husbands as individuals, even if we are displeased with their actions. Our words should separate their behavior from their identity—addressing their mistakes without diminishing their worth. Forgiveness does not mean accepting mistreatment or becoming a doormat. Scripture reminds us that God is just in His forgiveness, and likewise, we must pursue both grace and justice. A peaceful home cannot exist without accountability. We must communicate when we have been hurt in a way that facilitates healing rather than judgment.

Our humanity presents us with difficult tensions. We have the tendency to press for the extremes: being more or less than human. The truth is we are just plain human, and so are our husbands. We are both fallible, hence the need for forgiveness. When we embrace the truth of our own humanity, it ought to increase our capacity to forgive.

Forgiveness is not easy. It requires vulnerability, a willingness to release the pain and trust in God's protection rather than our own defense mechanisms. Sometimes we use unforgiveness as a shield against future hurt. However, true security lies in God, who is our refuge and strength. When we forgive our husbands, we align ourselves with His divine order, ensuring that our marriages are filled with grace, love, and restoration.

Scripture References:

- Luke 17:3-4
- 1 John 1:9
- Matthew 6:14-15
- Colossians 3:13
- Ephesians 4:31-32
- Mark 11:25
- 1 Peter 4:8
- Proverbs 17:9
- Romans 12:17-21

CHAPTER 4

LOVING OUR HUSBANDS UNCONDITIONALLY

Becoming a Student of Your Husband

One of the most profound ways to love our husbands unconditionally is to become students of them. This involves learning both directly and indirectly how we can best support, encourage, and nurture them as they pursue their God-given purpose.

We learn directly by engaging in meaningful conversations, asking them what they need, and creating a safe space where they feel comfortable expressing their desires and vulnerabilities. Open communication is key to understanding how we can be their partners in growth and success. However, not everything can or will be expressed in words. Many men struggle to articulate their emotional and spiritual needs, either because they are unaware of them or because they fear appearing weak. This is where indirect learning becomes crucial.

We observe their actions, their responses to life's challenges, their reactions to stress, and the things that bring them joy or discouragement. By doing this, we gain insight into their deepest needs, even when they cannot verbalize them. This requires patience, discernment, and an intentional commitment to study them over time. Proverbs 19:20 reminds us, "Listen to advice and accept discipline, and at the end, you will be counted among the wise." As wives, wisdom in loving our husbands begins with listening and observing.

Responding vs. Reacting

One of the greatest challenges in marriage is learning to respond rather than react. A reaction is immediate, often emotional, and sometimes based on incomplete information. A response, however, is measured, prayerful, and seeks to bring resolution rather than conflict.

To respond in love, we must take the time to:

1. **Gather the facts** – What actually happened versus how we perceived it?

2. **Consider different perspectives** – What might our husband be going through that led to this moment?

3. **Seek God's wisdom** – What response aligns with God's word and furthers unity rather than division?

James 1:19 advises, "Everyone should be quick to listen, slow to speak and slow to become angry." A simple but powerful phrase I learned to use in moments of tension is: "I'm on your team, and I love you madly." Expressing love and unity before addressing an issue can prevent many conflicts from escalating. This aligns with Philippians 2:3-4, which instructs us to consider others above ourselves. By prioritizing our husband's well-being and perspective, we align our hearts with Christ's love.

Loving Within the Boundaries of Righteousness

Loving unconditionally does not mean enabling ungodly behavior or compromising our Christian integrity. True love holds our husbands accountable to righteousness. We are their helpmates, not their enablers.

When our husband's desires or actions conflict with God's word, we must lovingly and respectfully stand firm in our convictions. Love does not mean blind submission to wrongdoing; rather, it means encouraging and supporting them in their spiritual growth. Proverbs 27:17 reminds us, "As iron sharpens iron, so one person sharpens another." Our love should refine, strengthen, and uplift, not simply conform to ease and comfort.

The Power of Unconditional Love

Unconditional love is not based on how our husbands act or respond but on our commitment to love them as Christ loves us. Jesus loves us despite our flaws, mistakes, and shortcomings. In the same way, we are called to love our husbands—not just when they meet our expectations, but even when they fall short.

This kind of love requires:

- **Grace** – Understanding that they, like us, are imperfect and in need of patience.

- **Forgiveness** – Letting go of offenses and choosing to see them through God's eyes.

- **Encouragement** – Speaking life and affirming their God-given potential.

- **Prayer** – Covering them in prayer daily, asking God to strengthen, lead, and guide them.

1 Peter 4:8 teaches, "Above all, love each other deeply, because love covers over a multitude of sins." Our husbands will make mistakes, just as we do. But if we commit to loving them unconditionally, we create a foundation of grace that strengthens our marriage.

Building a Christ-Centered Marriage

A marriage rooted in unconditional love is a testimony of Christ's love for the church. When we love our husbands with the selfless, sacrificial love that God calls us to, we create an environment where they can thrive.

Marriage is not about molding our husband into the "perfect mate" based on our ideals. Rather, it is about walking alongside them, helping them become the men God created them to be. It is about creating a relationship that reflects the love, grace, and mercy of Christ.

When we love our husbands unconditionally, we mirror the very love that God extends to us. It is through this love that marriages flourish, unity is strengthened, and God is glorified.

Scripture References:

- Proverbs 19:20
- James 1:19
- Philippians 2:3-4
- Proverbs 27:17
- 1 Peter 4:8

CHAPTER 5

REVERENCING
OUR HUSBANDS

As the heart of the home, it is imperative that women understand the importance of respect in the lives of their husbands. Respect is not just a preference for men—it is a core need. Scripture affirms this truth in Ephesians 5:33, where Paul commands, "However, each one of you also must love his wife as he loves himself, and the wife must respect her husband."

It is often said that men would rather be respected than loved, while women would rather be loved than respected. While this may not apply universally, it highlights an essential difference in how men and women tend to experience love. As wives, we are called upon to consider a perspective that is different from our own, and to love our husbands in the way that speaks most powerfully to them—through reverence and respect.

How Do We Reverence Our Husbands?

Reverencing our husbands is an intentional practice that must be demonstrated in both word and deed. Our words should build them up, affirming their worth and their God-given role in the home. Proverbs 31:26 tells us, "She speaks with wisdom, and faithful instruction is on her tongue." Even in moments of disappointment or frustration, we are still called to speak the truth in love (Ephesians 4:15). If we internalize the definition of love given in 1 Corinthians 13—love that is patient, kind, not easily angered, and keeps no record of wrongs—it will aid us in reverencing our husbands, even when it is difficult.

Respecting our husbands also requires us to align our priorities correctly. After God and self-care, our husbands should come next in importance—even before our children. While this may seem counterintuitive, a strong and godly marriage provides the most stable and nurturing environment for children. When a husband and wife function in unity, they create a foundation of security that benefits the entire household.

Demonstrating Respect in Daily Life

One of the most powerful ways to reverence our husbands is by being mindful of our responses. Our reactions can either encourage them or tear them down. Consider a story I once heard on a Christian radio program:

A wife had prepared a beautiful dinner for her husband, only for him to arrive home late without calling. The meal was ruined, and she was deeply disappointed. At this point, she faced a choice—she could unleash her frustration in anger, or she could communicate her feelings with love and respect. Because she valued her husband and their relationship, she chose the latter. She shared her disappointment honestly but without accusation. Instead of responding defensively, her husband apologized and took steps to be more mindful in the future.

Had she reacted in frustration, blaming and shaming him, where would the glory be for God in that? How would that option have built up her husband or demonstrated that she was the heart of the home? As we have already seen in Proverbs 14:1, "The wise woman builds her house, but with her own hands the foolish one tears hers down." Reverence means choosing words and actions that contribute to building a home rather than tearing it apart.

The Power of Respect in Strengthening a Marriage

Respect fosters an environment where love can flourish. My husband, Ron, used to say, "That does not endear you to me," when my actions or words hurt him. This phrase made me pause and reflect on how my behavior impacted our relationship. Once, when his demanding travel schedule left me feeling lonely and neglected, I faced a choice. Instead of complaining or accusing, I simply expressed my feelings. Because I communicated in a respectful and loving way, he responded with tenderness—dancing with me in a gas station parking lot to reassure me of his love. That moment became a cherished memory rather than a point of contention.

When we revere our husbands, we create an atmosphere where they feel safe to reciprocate with the love we desire. Respect begets love, just as love begets respect. When a husband knows he is honored and valued, he is far more likely to respond with affection, care, and devotion.

Overcoming the Challenge of Reverencing Our Husbands

If we struggle with respecting our husbands, we must examine our motivation. Many times, we miss the mark because we react based on what our husbands do or say rather than responding to who God has called us to be. This can lead to resentment, anger, and retaliation—none of which produce godly results. Instead, we should respond only to God's calling and His desire for us to be Christlike wives.

Jesus Himself modeled this principle. He did not respond in kind to insults or mistreatment; rather, He remained steadfast in His purpose. In 1 Peter 2:23, it says, "When they hurled their insults at him, he did not retaliate; when he suffered, he made no threats. Instead, he entrusted himself to him who judges justly." If we seek first His kingdom and His righteousness (Matthew 6:33), He will provide us with the wisdom, patience, forgiveness, and peace needed to live out our roles as wives who reverence their husbands.

Trusting God's Power Over Our Marriages

I know some may say, "But you don't know my husband." You are right—but I do know God. He is all-powerful, and His Spirit works in ways we cannot see. If we honor God by honoring our husbands, we invite His divine intervention into our marriages. Reverencing our husbands is not about ignoring faults or enduring mistreatment; rather, it is about fulfilling our God-given role with faith and obedience, trusting Him to shape and transform both our hearts and our husbands'.

Through reverence, we give God room to work in our marriages, and He is faithful to bless our obedience. As we respect our husbands in word and deed, we reflect Christ's love, build a strong foundation for our families, and glorify God in our marriages.

Scripture References:

- Ephesians 5:33
- Proverbs 31:26
- Ephesians 4:15
- 1 Corinthians 13:4-5
- Proverbs 14:1
- 1 Peter 2:23
- Matthew 6:33
- Song of Solomon 2:16

CHAPTER 6

FINANCIAL HARMONY –
A FOUNDATION FOR PEACE
IN MARRIAGE

F inancial harmony is one of the most important cornerstones of a peaceful, thriving marriage. When couples align in their financial values, priorities, and goals, they set the stage for unity—not just in money matters, but in every other area of their relationship.

Money is one of the leading causes of tension in marriages. Whether it is because of differing spending habits, hidden debt, or conflicting priorities, unresolved financial conflict can erode trust and intimacy. But when couples approach their finances with mutual respect, transparency, and a shared vision, they create not only financial stability but emotional safety.

Stewardship, Not Just Spending

At the heart of financial harmony is the principle of stewardship. As believers, we understand that everything we have belongs to God, and we are simply caretakers of His provision. This means we must handle our money with care, wisdom, and intentionality.

Proverbs 21:5 reminds us, "The plans of the diligent lead to profit as surely as haste leads to poverty." This verse captures a powerful truth: diligent planning and wise decision-making lead to fruitfulness. Hasty, emotional, or unexamined choices, on the other hand, can lead to financial strain—and ultimately, relational tension.

Mutual Decision-Making Builds Unity

When both spouses are actively engaged in financial decisions—big or small—they cultivate a spirit of unity. Financial conversations should not be dominated by one partner or avoided altogether. Instead, they should be regular, honest, and approached as a team.

Whether it is deciding on a monthly budget, saving for a home, giving to the church, or planning for a family vacation, every financial choice offers an opportunity to grow in understanding and connection. When both voices are heard and respected, each person feels valued. This strengthens trust and promotes mutual accountability.

Transparency Creates Safety

Secrets in finances are just as damaging as secrets in any other area of marriage. Hidden credit card bills, secret purchases, or undisclosed debts erode trust. Transparency—being open about income, expenses, goals, and fears—builds emotional safety.

Couples should regularly sit down to go over their finances together. These conversations are not just about money—they are about dreams, values, and hopes or fears for the future. Transparency invites vulnerability, and vulnerability invites deeper intimacy.

Practical Tools for Financial Harmony

To build financial peace in your marriage, consider incorporating the following tools and habits:

- **Budget Together:** Set monthly financial goals, track expenses, and celebrate wins together.

- **Pray About Financial Decisions:** Invite God into your planning. He provides wisdom and peace.

- **Assign Roles:** One partner may be better at handling day-to-day management, but both should remain informed.

- **Practice Generosity Together:** Tithing, giving, and blessing others fosters a spirit of abundance and trust in God's provision.

- **Seek Guidance:** Consider meeting with a financial advisor or taking a Christian financial stewardship class together.

Vision for the Future

A couple aligned in financial purpose walks in confidence. They can support one another's callings, prepare for the future, and model healthy financial habits for their children. When financial stress is minimized, couples are freed to focus on growing in love, purpose, and service.

Good communication is key in every area of our relationship with our husbands. The area of finances is no exception. As one flesh there should be no "mine" and "yours," but rather "ours," when it comes to finances. I recommend that couples make a full disclosure of all debts and financial obligations before they say "I do," and continue to practice being fully transparent throughout their marriage. Conversely, they should also list the assets held by each person.

Remember that in Genesis, when God brought Adam and Eve together, they were "naked and not ashamed." This means they were vulnerable and transparent with each other. We need to know if we are like-minded on the subject of money or polar opposites. Is one of us a spender and the other a saver? Does one believe in risky investment and the other leans more conservative? Remember that the goal is to be of one accord, so be willing to work to understand your husband's position and compromise together when it is the right thing to do.

Couples should also have a budget that assists them in making sure all household expenses are met, as well as planning for the future. The first step is to determine what the current expenses are. The budget not only includes household expenses but also savings, investments, vacations, and leisure activities.

Some Practical Recommendations

I generally recommend that couples use the following guidelines: 10% tithes, 10% savings, 10% investment, and 70% living expenses. In the 70%, money can be set aside for each spouse as discretionary, a certain spending amount determined by lifestyle needs. For example, if one person's hobby is tennis and the other's is golf, one may need more allowance in the discretionary fund than the other. For couples looking to examine their budgeting and spending more deeply, I recommend Dave Ramsey's Financial Peace University, which instructs couples on how to live debt-free.

Couples need to agree together on how to divide financial duties. Often, this task may be assigned to the husband by default. However, I recommend having a discussion as to which person is more suited to handle the finances. Even after a budget has been agreed upon, there still needs to be agreement on who decides to enact it or act as the financial secretary. Being the head of the home does not mean the husband must make all the financial decisions alone and do the entirety of the bookkeeping. These should be shared responsibilities. The most important factor is to ensure that both parties feel heard, so they can come to a mutual agreement.

Couples can then work together to determine their short-term and long-term financial goals. Be sure to include in your discussion of finances the topic of wills, living trusts, and pre-need arrangements. Couples should research, discuss, and purchase insurance for both parties. A good rule to follow in terms of life insurance is to obtain enough coverage for the surviving spouse to live one year without having to make any changes to their lifestyle due to finances.

Finances can be stressful, but there is so much growth that can take place as a couple plans and executes their financial future together. Let your financial life be a testimony of God's order and provision. Be diligent, be generous, and be unified. A couple walking in financial harmony becomes a powerful force for good—building not just a house, but a home anchored in peace, purpose, and prosperity.

Scripture References:

- Proverbs 21:5
- Malachi 3:6-12
- Proverbs 31
- Matthew 6:25-33

CHAPTER 7

A ROLE MODEL
OF GOD-LIKENESS

The Role of a Godly Wife

A wife's role in the home is sacred. She is called to be a reflection of Christ's love, grace, and wisdom. The Bible provides clear guidance on how she should relate to her husband, modeling godliness through her character and conduct. 1 Peter 3:1-6 highlights that a wife has the power to influence her husband, even an unbelieving one, not through nagging or forceful words but through a spirit of gentleness, purity, and reverence.

Submission: A Reflection of Trust and Respect

As we discussed earlier, submission is one of the most misunderstood biblical principles. Many view it as oppressive, yet biblically, submission is a sign of strength, trust, and obedience to God. Just as Christ submitted to the Father's will (Philippians 2:5-8), wives are called to submit to their husbands as an act of reverence for God's divine order (Ephesians 5:22-25). This submission is not about inferiority or blind obedience but about acknowledging the husband's God-given role as the leader of the home.

However, a husband's role is equally significant. He is commanded to love his wife sacrificially, just as Christ loved the church (Ephesians 5:25). When a husband leads with love, humility, and integrity, submission becomes a natural response rather than a struggle.

Inner Beauty Over Outward Adornment

The Bible repeatedly emphasizes that true beauty is found in the heart. Proverbs 31:30 states, "Charm is deceptive, and beauty is fleeting; but a woman who fears the Lord is to be praised." While there is nothing wrong with caring for one's appearance, the priority should always be the cultivation of a gentle and quiet spirit—one that is at peace, full of wisdom, and deeply rooted in faith.

A godly wife's beauty radiates through her kindness, patience, and wisdom. This inner beauty not only strengthens her marriage but also serves as a testimony to others, drawing them closer to God.

Purity and Reverence in Conduct

A wife's conduct should reflect her reverence for God and her commitment to holiness. Jesus said, "Out of the overflow of the heart, the mouth speaks" (Luke 6:45). Therefore, a wife should fill her heart with God's Word and cultivate virtues that reflect Christ's love.

Key aspects of godly conduct include:

- **Speaking words of encouragement** – "A gentle answer turns away wrath, but a harsh word stirs up anger" (Proverbs 15:1).

- **Practicing patience and kindness** – "Clothe yourselves with compassion, kindness, humility, gentleness, and patience" (Colossians 3:12).

- **Demonstrating grace and forgiveness** – "Be kind and compassionate to one another, forgiving each other, just as in Christ God forgave you" (Ephesians 4:32).

Trusting God to Lead Your Husband

One of the greatest challenges wives face is trusting their husbands to lead, especially when they fear mistakes or uncertainty. However, God is always in control. Just as He refines a wife's faith, He also works in her husband's heart.

To cultivate trust:

- **Release control and allow God to guide your husband.**

- **Pray for wisdom and patience (James 1:5).**

- **Encourage and support his role rather than criticize.**

Stormie Omartian's book *The Power of a Praying Wife* is an excellent resource for wives seeking to intercede effectively for their husbands.

Resisting the Enemy Through Obedience

The enemy seeks to destroy marriages by sowing discord, pride, and resentment. James 4:7 teaches, "Submit yourselves, then, to God. Resist the devil, and he will flee from you." When a wife submits to God and His design for marriage, she strengthens her home against the enemy's attacks.

By resisting the temptation to control, retaliate, or act out of anger, a wife fortifies her home's spiritual foundation. The battle is not won through force but through faith, patience, and obedience to God's will.

Building a Spirit-Filled Home

A home filled with the Holy Spirit becomes a sanctuary of peace, love, and faith. Galatians 5:22-23 describes the fruit of the Spirit: love, joy, peace, patience, kindness, goodness, faithfulness, gentleness, and self-control. A wife who embodies these qualities will create an environment where mutual respect and love flourish.

Allowing Your Husband to Cover You

A godly husband serves as a spiritual covering for his wife, just as Christ is the head of the church (Ephesians 5:23). This covering includes:

- **Physical protection** – Ensuring the well-being and safety of his family.

- **Emotional support** – Being a source of encouragement and strength.

- **Spiritual leadership** – Leading in prayer, worship, and godly decision-making.

Trusting God's process means allowing a husband to grow into this role, even when the journey is imperfect. James 1:2-4 reminds us that trials produce endurance and maturity.

Conclusion: A Wife's First Ministry

A wife's most important ministry is her home. Through submission, purity, trust, and prayer, she becomes a beacon of godliness in her household. Instead of focusing on changing her husband, she should focus on her own spiritual growth, setting an example that invites transformation.

True beauty is found in a woman who walks in the Spirit and builds a home filled with love, peace, and faith. When a wife embraces her divine role, her marriage becomes a testimony of God's grace and order.

Scripture References:

- 1 Peter 3:1-6
- Philippians 2:5-8
- Ephesians 5:22-25
- Proverbs 31:30
- Luke 6:45
- Proverbs 15:1.
- Colossians 3:
- Ephesians 4:32
- James 1:5
- James 4:7
- Galatians 5:22-
- Ephesians 5:23
- James 1:2-4

CHAPTER 8

CONCLUSION: BUILDING A CHRIST-CENTERED MARRIAGE

As we draw to the conclusion of this journey, we now reflect on the transformative steps and insights we have explored. The foundation of a thriving, Christ-centered marriage is built upon key principles—honoring, loving, respecting, and communicating effectively. This final chapter serves to summarize the core lessons from each of the previous chapters, reinforcing the wisdom shared for cultivating a marriage that reflects God's love and grace.

Chapter 1: Communications from the Heart

Communication is the heart of a successful marriage. The ability to speak and listen with respect, love, and understanding is essential to resolving conflicts and deepening connections. As we learned, the key to good communication is to respect one another, listen actively, and speak the truth in love, as described in **Ephesians 4:15**. When both partners communicate from a place of love and humility, they create an atmosphere of trust and openness, allowing the marriage to thrive.

Chapter 2: Building our Husbands Up

We began by understanding that honoring our husbands is an act of obedience to God's command. It is not about agreeing with everything he does but recognizing his God-given role in the marriage. By respecting his leadership, we create an environment where both partners can flourish. A wife's respect is one of the greatest gifts she can offer, and this honor is deeply rooted in Scripture, as seen in passages like **Ephesians 5:33**: "However, each one of you also must love his wife as he loves himself, and the wife must respect her husband."

Chapter 3: The Covenant of Marriage and Forgiveness

The essence of love in marriage, as outlined in **1 Corinthians 13:4-7**, is selfless and sacrificial. Love that endures all things, believes all things, and hopes all things is the cornerstone of a strong marriage. By choosing to love unconditionally, we mirror the love Christ has for us, which empowers both partners to weather any storm. We explored how choosing to love despite differences is a powerful testament to God's grace in our lives.

Chapter 4: Loving our Husbands Unconditionally

Submission in marriage is not about inferiority or subjugation, but a voluntary and loving choice to support our husbands' leadership. **Ephesians 5:22-24** teaches that wives are to submit to their husbands as the church submits to Christ. This submission is a mutual exchange of love, trust, and commitment to the well-being of each other. True submission is rooted in mutual respect and trust in God's divine design.

Chapter 5: Reverencing Our Husbands

Respect between spouses is not optional; it is a fundamental requirement for a thriving relationship. As **1 Peter 3:7** reminds us, husbands are to treat their wives with respect, understanding that they are co-heirs with them of the gracious gift of life. Respect fosters peace, strengthens emotional intimacy, and builds a marriage on a solid foundation. This chapter emphasized how the lack of respect undermines the ability to love deeply and communicate effectively.

Chapter 6: Financial Harmony – A Foundation for Peace in Marriage

Financial harmony is critical for maintaining peace and unity in marriage. In this chapter, we explored how wise financial stewardship, mutual decision-making, and transparent communication about money can reduce stress and strengthen the relationship. **Proverbs 21:5** tells us, "The plans of the diligent lead to profit as surely as haste leads to poverty." A couple who works together on financial goals builds trust, accountability, and a shared vision for the future.

Chapter 7: A Role Model of God-likeness

A wife's role in the home is sacred. She is called to be a reflection of Christ's love, grace, and wisdom. The Bible provides clear guidance on how she should relate to her husband, modeling godliness through her character and conduct. **1 Peter 3:1-6** highlights that a wife has the power to influence her husband, even an unbelieving one, not through nagging or forceful words but through a spirit of gentleness, purity, and reverence.

Chapter 8: Final Thoughts: Building a Christ-Centered Marriage

In closing, we recognize that a successful, Christ-centered marriage is not the result of striving for perfection, but of growing together in love, respect, and trust. Every step toward deepening our connection with our husbands is a step closer to fulfilling God's purpose for our marriage. Remember, **Colossians 3:14** reminds us that above all, we must "put on love, which binds everything together in perfect harmony."

As wives, we are called to be our husbands' helpers, encouragers, and greatest supporters. We honor God by honoring our husbands and embracing the roles He has designed for us. By cultivating love, communication, respect, and mutual understanding, we can build marriages that reflect His glory and embody His teachings.

May God bless your marriage with deep love, unwavering respect, and His perfect peace as you continue to walk together, hand in hand, through the journey of life.

Prayer: Lord, thank You for the gift of marriage and for the opportunity to reflect Your love through our relationships. Help us to be faithful, loving, and respectful wives, guided by Your Word in all we do. Teach us how to communicate effectively, love unconditionally, and support our husbands as they lead our homes. May our marriages be a testament to Your goodness and grace. In Jesus' name, Amen.

COUPLE OR GROUP QUESTIONS FOR REFLECTION AND DISCUSSION

These questions are designed to spark meaningful conversations and reflections, either between you and your spouse or in a group setting. They are intended to help deepen your understanding of the principles shared in each chapter, fostering growth and connection in your relationship.

Introduction: The Call to Honor Your Husband

1. How can you show your husband honor in ways that align with his personality and preferences, rather than just your own expectations?

2. In what ways have you struggled with honoring your husband, and what steps can you take to address this issue with love and humility?

Chapter 1: Communications from the Heart

1. Ask your spouse: How can we improve our communication by actively listening and speaking with kindness, even when we disagree?

2. What are some specific examples of what a "safe" environment for open and honest conversations looks like in our marriage?

Chapter 2: Building Our Husbands Up

1. Can you recall a time when you showed unconditional love to your spouse? How did it impact your relationship?

2. What are some challenges you and your spouse face in loving unconditionally, and how can you work together to overcome them, particularly when you disagree?

Chapter 3: The Covenant of Marriage and Forgiveness

1. What does submission look like in your relationship, and how can you ensure it is mutual and rooted in respect for each other?

2. How can you and your husband both support one another in fulfilling our God-given roles in the marriage without feeling threatened or undermined?

Chapter 4: Loving our Husbands Unconditionally

1. Ask your spouse: How can we create a safe space in our relationship where we both feel comfortable sharing our deepest thoughts and feelings without fear of judgment?

2. What are some small, everyday actions we can take to build emotional intimacy and strengthen our connection with each other?

Chapter 5: Reverencing our Husbands

1. What specific behaviors or actions can you both adopt to ensure that you always show each other respect in your marriage?

2. How do you respond when you feel disrespected by one another, and how can you address these feelings constructively?

Chapter 6: Financial Harmony – A Foundation for Peace in Marriage

1. What are some common financial challenges you face as a couple, and how can you work together to resolve them with integrity and wisdom?

2. How can you create a financial plan that honors God and aligns with your shared goals as a couple, both short-term and long-term?

Chapter 7: A Role Model of God-likeness

1. In what ways does our relationship reflect God's love, grace, and forgiveness toward each other.

2. How are we modeling mutual submission and respect as taught in Scripture, and how does that impact our home environment?

Chapter 8: Building A Christ-Centered Marriage

As you reflect on these questions, consider the ways you can strengthen your marriage by applying the principles from each chapter. Take time to listen to one another, share openly, and encourage each other in your journey together. Building a strong marriage takes intentional effort, prayer, and a willingness to grow together as partners in Christ.

REVEREND JOYCE REECE KITCHEN

Rev. Joyce Reece Kitchen is the Pastor of Emmanuel - Henry McNeal Turner African Methodist Episcopal Church. However, being a pastor is just one expression of her commitment to service. For over seventeen years, Rev. Kitchen worked as a Physician's Assistant, a Master's Degree-level position, where she witnessed firsthand the incredible emotional pain and sicknesses that polluted the lives of many families she serviced. While in this capacity she embraced the opportunity to improve the quality of her client's lives physically, emotionally, and spiritually. Many young parents looked to Rev. Kitchen as a "surrogate mother," as she taught them how to effectively care for their children and improve their life situations.

In 1997, at the ripe age of forty-two, Rev. Kitchen left this comfortable, high-paying career and returned to school, once again embracing her commitment to service and God's will for her talents. Two years later, she received her Master's Degree in Social Welfare from the University of California, Los Angeles (UCLA), and began working for the Los Angeles County Department of Children and Family Services, Adoptions Unit. There she helped abused children find families to love and care for them.

With the passing of her late husband, Rev. Ronald Johnson, her son, Rev. Charles Lee Johnson, picked up the mantle to finish his father's work by assuming the position of CEO of the nonprofit agency National Family & Life Center (NFLEC), a vibrant institution created by his father. Recognizing the immense challenge facing her very young but determined son, Rev. Kitchen accepted the position of COO and assisted Rev. Charles in expanding the foundation's national and international work. At NFLEC, Rev. Kitchen provided a myriad of services, including Human Resources, employee supervision, and direct client services, such as transitional housing for emancipated foster children under the age of 18. The agency had a 90% graduation rate for its students, with many continuing on to pursue higher education.

Given her ability to integrate professional knowledge with her faith, Rev. Kitchen is highly respected in both the ecumenical and secular communities. As a facilitator for co-dependency groups and a Licensed Clinical Social Worker, Rev. Kitchen counsels individuals and couples throughout the nation, who appreciate her ability to "tell it like it is." Using a gentle but firm approach, she speaks to the heart of people's hurt, helping them to transition from pain to power. Truly anointed by God, she excels in marital counseling and is known as a prayer warrior who has taught numerous dynamic workshops on the power of prayer.

Born and raised in Los Angeles, Rev. Joyce Kitchen earned her Bachelor's degree in Sociology from the University of Southern California (USC), a Bachelor's degree in Health Science from California State University at Dominguez Hills (CSUDH), and a P.A. Certification from Charles R. Drew Postgraduate Medical School. Rev. Kitchen is the wife of Award-Winning Advertising Writer/Producer and Playwright, Maurice Kitchen, who also founded the popular a cappella singing group, Street Corner Renaissance. She is the mother of five children, the grandmother of eleven, and the great-grandmother of three. Rev. Joyce Reece Kitchen, a determined soldier on the battlefield for Christ and her community, continues to fight the good fight. To God be the glory.

www.ingramcontent.com/pod-product-compliance
Lightning Source LLC
Chambersburg PA
CBHW050907120626
46554CB00003B/1053